On Eagles Wings -
A Journey Takes Flight
Poems for Heart and Soul

By
Juliana Peter

Illustrated by
Jill Benson Flanagan

On Eagles Wings – A Journey Takes Flight
Poems for Heart and Soul

Illustrations by Jill Benson Flanagan
Front cover photo by John Dakin

ISBN: 1721766944
ISBN-13: 978-1721766949

Contents

DEDICATION

This book is dedicated to my
late sister-in-law, Ella.

ACKNOWLEDGMENTS

Many poets write with inspiration received from others. A special thank you to Fr. Patrick Dolan, Pastor, Most Precious Blood Church. On many occasions, his homilies were the inspiration that started the thought process which led to a poem. "We are Gift," "The Desert or the Cross," and "We are Community" are just a few poems that began in the pew, and then were translated into poetry.

Thanks to my spiritual directors, Andy Drance and Kyle Turner who encouraged me on my journey as it took flight.

A very special acknowledgement to Jill Benson Flanagan, illustrator. Jill went beyond illustrating poems, she created illustrations that inspired poems. "Precipice," "In Over my Head," and "Year by Year" are a few poems her illustrations inspired. Her illustrations are all drawn from her own internal inspiration. This book has been years in the making; thank you for your patience on this journey.

I'm glad my life path crossed with John Dakin. John's nature photography captures the beauty of its subjects. Thanks for the cover photo.

A very special thanks to my husband, Francis. You played the role of technical advisor, coach, and number one fan for the project. Without you, this book would not have been published.

Introduction

It was an ordinary day. The sun was shining as it often does in Colorado. The errands requiring attention were quite ordinary on this very ordinary day.

As I drove westward along Hwy. 6, my mind focused on the next errand before heading home. The Eagle River bubbling with early Spring runoff reminded of warmer days to come. Then, out of nowhere, there appeared a majestic bald eagle. He, too, was facing West, intently following the Eagle River downstream. Expecting him to dive for a fish, I thought his appearance would be brief.

But, no! He flew in perfect cadence, he on wings and me in my car. We were in sync. He did not lose me, nor I him.

Then, as though giving me a message, these words emerged, "on the wings of eagles." The phrase reverberated over and over in my mind. Then he was gone, but the words remained.

As time passed, these words and this image remained fixed in my mind's eye and sealed in my heart's desire. Many months passed before I wrote the first poem. In the weeks that followed the initial poems, more poems emerged on paper from the pen held loosely in my hand.

As the days, weeks and months followed, I thought little of the poetry, but after many months something bubbled within. I began to share the poems with others. Almost universally I received positive comments. Thoughts of publishing began to fill the blank spaces in the mind. I then asked a friend, Jill Benson Flanagan, if she would be interested in creating illustrations. She agreed. And the project was launched. However, progress was slow. It took years instead of months. Finally, the drive to run (or was it fly?) with the plans to publish overtook the nagging doubts.

The eagle who flew with me that day several years ago returned to mind's eye. I flew forward, borne up by those wings to share with you, dear reader, my journey. Enjoy the poems within. And may you, too, mount up on eagle's wings.

Section I:

Provisions on the Journey

Everlasting Arms

Everlasting arms
    Supporting
    Protecting
    Engulfing our being

Loving as a mother's warm embrace
Guiding like a caring father
Shielding us from arrows by day and pestilence by night
Providing sustenance under the burning noon day sun
Giving refreshing water from cool mountain springs
Sustaining as rocks crumble under foot

Yes, everlasting arms
    Strong
    Unyielding to evil's devouring desires
Everlasting arms stretched out on a cross;
Feeding us with sweet blood of forgiveness

Everlasting arms bring
    Comfort in grief
    Hope in disappointment
    Love in moments of aloneness

Your Hands

Your hands touched the centurion's daughter
     raising her from the dead
Your hands touched the Prodigal
     welcoming him home
Your hands hugged little children
     "let the little ones come"
Your hands covered with splinters
     carrying the cross
Your hands pierced by nails
     driven by Roman soldiers

Hands of love
Hands of compassion
Hands of healing
Hands that bled
Hands that welcome us home

We place our hands into yours to receive
     Peace
     Rest
     Love

We walk hand in hand with you
     Resting
     Trusting
     Knowing peace

Follow the Passion

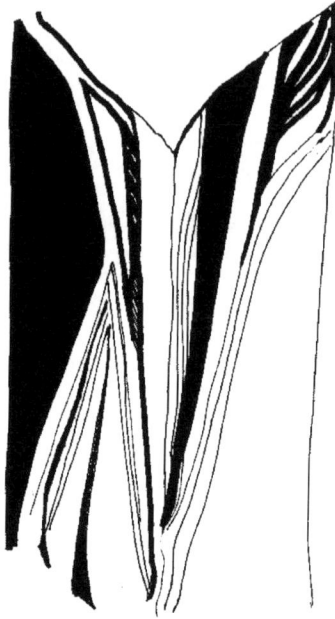

We are a temple
His temple
Within the heart He desires to dwell
Dwelling
     To create an abundant life
     To create beauty
     To create a vision to serve

His dwelling conveys journey
To inspire the spark that lights the flame
To light the lamp for others

Buy my soul is in dormant state
The soul does not give His presence recognition

My core recognizes naught His desire for me
A shift occurs; sudden and sure
Recognition comes; desire is awakened
An assured voice sings in unison with my soul
Create as I have created
I will give you
> Food to eat
> Water to drink
> A place to dwell

With definition He speaks,
My desire will be your desire.
Your desire will be united with mine.

Together we create
> Beauty with the stroke of a brush
> Cacophony from an orchestra tuned
> Healing words from ancient age's wisdom
> Sculptures from marble to soften hardened hearts
> Joyful dance to rhythm of tambourine

Passion alive within
Pay homage to His indwelling presence
Rejoice
Live fully
With passion

Lead Us

Eternal Spirit, direct our path
Shine light on journey's road
Guide us with your eye

Lead us with Truth
Lead us to the perfect Way
That we may receive
>   Revelation
>   Direction
>   Wisdom
Our paths – we do not see the end
We cannot see beyond today
We see not beyond our present moment
But we do see victory gained
We see the end result
Being held in the loving arms of the Word all the way

Crossing Jordan

Step by step
Crossing Jordan
Into a land of milk and honey
Houses are built and furnished
  Ready for possession
Wells are dug
  Ready to supply everlasting drink
Vineyards are planted
  Producing grapes for celebratory wine
Orchards – ancient and yielding
  Olives for finest oil
  Oil to anoint
  Oil of gladness to bring rest to the heart
Honey – rich and sweet on the comb
Milk flowing for nourishment
Crossing Jordan
Step by step

Sons and Daughters

Sons and Daughters are we
Precious in your sight
Bought by sacrificial price
Ultimate sacrifice
> Betrayed
> Abandoned
> Suffering
> Broken
> Blood
Purchased by life poured out
> No higher ransom could be paid
> Not with silver
> Not with gold
How precious we appear
You call us by name
You call us by relationship
> Sons and Daughters
Precious in your sight
More than redeemed
Princes and Princesses, are we
Not to glory in self,
> but humbled by blood's ransom paid
We reflect
> Eternal relationship
We sing, voices raised
> Giving praise
> Proclaiming thanksgiving
> Honoring you
For an inheritance bestowed by grace and mercy
Sons and Daughters are we!

Blessings

Blessings come
Unexpectedly
Blessings come from the Father's bounty
 Daily manna upon desert floor
 Oil and flour for prophet and widow
 Five loaves and two fishes
Abundance pours forth
Blessings for asking
Blessings for receiving
A rich inheritance given to sons and daughters
Drink from the cup that never empties
Feast from table's cornucopia
Abundance abounds
Blessings pour out
Receive abundance
Be full and thirst not

Do not horde
Do not keep
Give from bounty
Your table will be replenished
Never to hunger or thirst again

The Journey

New day dawns, full of hope
New journey awaits in the wings of the unknown
Joyful anticipation swells within the breast
Let heart be your guide
As wisdom is your map

For you will have
       New roads to build
       New streams to cross
       New mountains to scale

Take courage
Nourishment has been provided
Drink wine from the chalice of gladness
Sup at the table of connection
Be anointed with sweet oils of healing
Taste the elixir of love

Look not back
Be in the moment of joy
And give thanks for the journey ahead

At the Foot of the Cross

At the foot of the cross
We seek
      Mercy
      Grace
      Acceptance

At the foot of the cross
We find
      Compassion
      Love
      Forgiveness
Mingled with water and blood

At the foot of the cross
We gaze upward
Blood shed
Wounds open and raw
All for us
      World's salvation
      Sinners and saints drawn together
      All given life
      Death departs
      No more thirst

We now are one
      Sweet communion cup
      Loved and blessed
      This day in Paradise

At the foot of the cross
Love came down
      Amazing love
      Divine gift
      Mercy and grace
Never ending life

Your Presence

Your presence comes to us
>In the still small voice
>Or in silence
>Sometimes in manifestation
>Bringing comfort
>Always to guide

You never leave us
You never forsake us
Forgive us for the times we feel
>Abandoned
>Rejected
>Despondent
>Doubtful
>Indifferent

Help us to move forward with faith
Not leaning into feelings
So we may experience your presence by possessing
>Faith
>Hope
>Love

The Perfect Way

In lament, Yours is the glory
In sorrow, Yours is the honor
In disappointment, Yours is the joy

My soul despairs
My heart quickens
For in you comes the assuring voice
Thanksgiving is on my lips
Not for the better way, but the perfect way

The perfect way revealed unexpectedly
In answers unimagined
In provision beyond imagination

Wait to see the perfect way
    Hope
    Peace
    Trust
Flooding the soul
Giving thanks for the perfect way

Gratitude

Thank you Spirit for your presence
For everlasting hand on shoulder
For protecting shadow covering soul
For loving arms bringing comfort
For intercession to the Father –
  Praying in unison with the Son

Holy Trinity bestowing only the best
For guiding light
For sending comfort
  In hour of disappointment
  In hour of grief and sorrow
  In hour of sadness

Holy Trinity
Working as one
Mysterious three in one
Pouring out blessings
Do we miss opportunity to enter the divine dance?

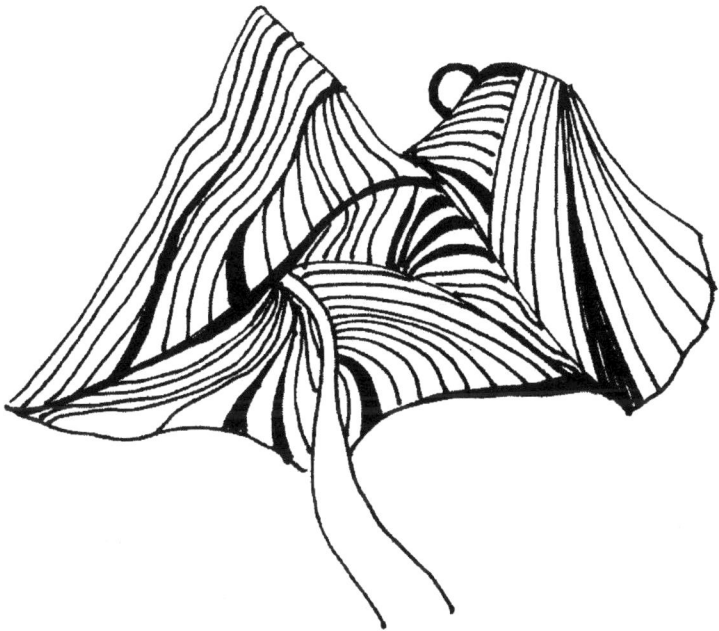

Roots and Wings

Roots burrowing into soil
Seeking nourishment and sending it forth
Tangled webs in quest for water
Friends with dark life residing in earth
Deeper and deeper
Wider and wider
Giving stability
Providing strength to stand tall
Unbending to wind
Sustaining life above the darkness

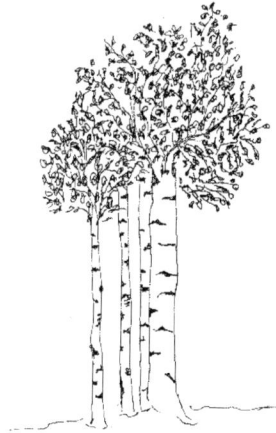

As bird rises to sky
May our wings
      Rise above the ordinary
      Sustain us on the journey
      Raise us up on the winds of hope

As we rise up
      To seek justice for the betrayed
      Give sustenance to the poor
          Poor in body or spirit
      Embrace the sojourner
      Pour grace and compassion on the prisoner
      Clothe the naked

Tree standing strong
Bark ever expanding
Clothed in colors
Bearing fruit
Giving shade
Bathing in golden sun rays
Rejoicing in rain
Casting shadow in full moon's light
Resting haven for creatures great and small

Tree of life
> Giving substance to all resting in our shadow
> Succor to those seeking rest
> Comfort to the weeping
> Friendship to the lonely
> Encouragement to the discouraged

May our roots
> Firmly ground us
> Accept nourishment
> Be intertwined with truth and justice
> Seek deeper ground
> Never be blinded by darkness

Roots
> Grounded in compassion and love
> Seeking truth and justice
> Nourished by Spirit
> Light in darkness

Truth

Truth is like a dove
Takes flight
Borne up by wings
Borne up on air beneath
Gracefully taking flight upward
Then descending
Speaking
Revealing with quiet words
Words unspoken
Words not discerned by language
Words of the Spirit
Known within
Only for a brief second
Then rises to the sky
Not to be held
But to be known for all time

Section II:

Crossroads on the Journey

See My Face

Calling out in the night
    "Show me the path"
Silence descends
    Cold
    Black
    Unyielding
Deserted and adrift am I
"Guiding Spirit, show me the path"

Deafening silence
Is there no path to trod upon?
Will silence be my daily bread?
Life without purpose?
Hollow existence?

Quietly, but with certainty
Sound of gentle footsteps touching soft earth
No apparition appears
But Gentle Spirit is there without form

Encouraged
More determined
"Gentle Spirit, show me purpose."
Steps coming closer
Spirit's tender presence revealed

Black silence is gone
Cold silence has ebbed
Waiting for Spirit's revelation

Lips tremble
"I will go where you lead"
Footsteps closer
Fostering peace
Imparting mysterious joy
Peace and joy – powerful duo

Sensing revelation
  Heart swells with anticipation
  Trust Gentle Spirit

Night moves forward
Dawn breaks
Gentle Spirit speaks,
"Heal the broken hearted."

Muddled
Looking through smoked glass
  Unsure
  Stunned
  But how?

"See my likeness imprinted on the face of every soul you
encounter."

Faith?

Faith alone?
Faith without response to need
Can it be?

What does faith require?
Can faith be felt?
Emotions run high
Feeling, not knowing
Feeling blessed
      We recite incantations of emotional highs
God moves in our midst and we feel the presence
      We call ourselves blessed

But like prairie grass that withers with autumn's cool arrival
Life shifts to loss
      Tragedies
      Broken relationships
      Aging
      Illness
      Fortune spent

Incantations shift from praise to asking
Believing faith will be honored
Hearts bent on receiving blessing
Blessing does not come in desired form

Emotions fall to blackening depths
Emotional high dissolves into vapor
The vapors rise
The vapors vanish
Emotional joy gone

Faith ebbs
        Mournful soul
        Tear-filled nights
        Broken hearted
        Sadness
        Grief

Is faith gaged by emotional response?
Is it expecting God to honor incantations?
Is it receiving God's love in all forms?

Emotion we feel your sting
Faith where is your bond?
Surrender comes
New faith sustains
Thanksgiving is offered
We are content

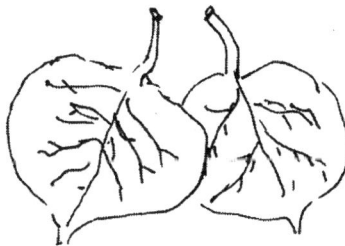

The Desert or the Cross

What desert of choice shall I enter
  One of self-sacrifice?
  One of focused discipline?
  One of giving to others?

To avoid the desert is to avoid the opportunity
  To grow
  To learn
  To become fully alive
  To be engaged with life
  To embrace the journey

The cross will be given to me
  Illness
  Friends lost
  Children gone astray
  Financial ruin
  Love departed

But when I traverse the desert
  I must glean daily provision
  I learn from lessons found in the oasis of hope
  Trust becomes my daily bread

When asked to carry the cross, I will be resolute
Yielding to its cleansing power to experience
  Freedom
  Strength
  Resurrection

Silence

In silence mind wanders
　　Bring it back
　　Only to wander again
　　Focus gone

But heart desires communion
Mind requires discipline
Heart and mind diverge
The call rings out
　　Come back
Mind hears the call
Responds for a few brief moments
"Come back" repeats the call
This time mind responds and stays moments longer
Heart rejoices for devoted time with Spirit

The discipline continues
The heart rejoices at the anticipation of union with mind

Time progresses
The two: heart and mind
Desire to be joined
But skirmish ensues
Can heart and mind become one?

Can heart's desire encircle mind's discipline?
Can mind's discipline surrender to heart's desire?
At intersection, the two touch
Truce is declared
Dichotomy does not rein
Each surrendering to the other

Mind disciplined, wanders less
Heart's desire burns with warm glow
Two become one
United
Soul
      Refreshed
      Renewed
      Blessed

In Over My Head

The Red Sea in front
Mountains to my left
Mountains to my right
Enemy bearing down

No boats to cross the sea
No horses to scale the mountains
No weapons to fight

Trapped
Death sits at the doors – ready to devour with glee

I kneel
Where is the victory?
Ready to yield to death's horrifying grip

"Touch the water" is whispered
"Cannot be," I respond
Gently, but with urging comes the words,
"Touch the water"
Can it be?
But what would come of that?
"Touch the water" comes a third time

Timidly the hand touches the water
The roar comes – a mighty wind
The water swirls
The waves heap up
Higher and higher the waves arise

The wind does not cease
Before me – not just a path
      But dry land
      Can it be?
One foot steps on dry land
Then another step is taken
"No need to rush," comes the reassuring voice

Step by step on dry land
Where once a formidable sea blocked entrance to freedom
Step by step
To the opposite shore I arrive

I turn
The wind stops
Waves of water crashing down
Covering the dry path
The sea returns to calm
Safely I turn to the journey ahead

Where are you God?

My soul cries out
Give ear to my lament
My soul sags within my breast
    Disheartened
    Discouraged
    Disconnected
Distance of magnitude unable to bear
Tears flow
Heaving with each breath
"Where is my God?"
Not a shadow seen
Not a whisper heard
Not a presence of Spirit felt

Do I walk?
Do I wait?
Do I create a plan?

What lies ahead?
    Are there barren valleys?
    Are there rock-strewn mountains?
    Or swift moving streams – impossible to ford?

Oh, for a drink of everlasting water
Oh, for manna poured out upon the ground for picking
I know not your presence
How will your hand guide?
How is it possible for your presence to direct my path?

Questions continue
Petitions spring forth
    Show me the way
    Give me a wisdom-filled map
    Provide the direction

My heart is still
With each slow beat
I wait with anticipation
Will you visit today?
Will I know your presence?
Will I experience your presence?
What will you be?

The sun rises
Light for a new day
Your presence comes
Soft as a gentle breeze
Manna for soul
Living water to quench heart's thirst
Steady hand guides
Watchful eye leads
All will be well

Precipice

On the move
Day and night
Night and day
Driven by burning desires
 More love
  Greater accomplishment
  Surefooted security
  Communal acceptance
  Unbound freedom

No day mirrors another
Challenge of victory seen, but not attained
Intoxicated by a moment won
Conflict rises to drain spirit
Love cushions
Untethered freedom flees

Never losing sight of desires, the journey continues
Wanting to grasp the brass ring drives journey onward
Desire consumes soul

Unexpected
Without premonition's tingle
Comes precipice

Journey halts

Precipice's undaunting strength
Echoes like a silent scream
Mind comprehends – road has ended

Fear mingles in muscles taut
Anxiety springs within the breast
Insecurity delivers muddle to the soul

Turn back from whence I came?
The road I know well
Marked by
       Pinnacles
       Valleys
       Rivers
       Fields of wheat
       Orchards bearing sweet fruit

The road I know well
       Flowers of spring
       Warm summer rains
       Cool colorful autumn days
       Unblemished snow sparking in full moon's light

The road I know well
       Silent lightning streaking before thunder's crackle
       Unrelenting wind
       Sun scorching landscape
       Crops diminished by drought
       Icy roads with no traction

Precipice
       Are you teacher or test?
       Are you guide or obstacle?
       Are you friend in disguise or foe revealed?

Voices swirl
Memories mingle on the dance floor of the mind
Echoes from the distant past compete for soul's allegiance

Inaudible sound offers doubt
Bound the precipice is to risk
    Failure
    Plunge into the abyss
    Cut off from life

Fear's vice grips tighter
    The unknown
    The unrevealed
    The taunting doubts

Hindsight viewing
Mind observing
Heart discerning
    Love is fleeting
    Accomplishment is envied, not admired
    Security is bundled in a thread worn cloak
    Acceptance is soup de jour
    Freedom is a hologram

A gentle breeze reveals a presence sensed
    "I, Eternal Spirit, will hold you by the hand"
    "I, Eternal Spirit, will bear you in flight"
    "I, Eternal Spirit, will not let you go"

Betwixt

Retreat or risk?

Doubt urges caution
        Remain with the known
Hope calls
        Action forward
        Faith engaged
        Believe

Trust eternal spirit's hand

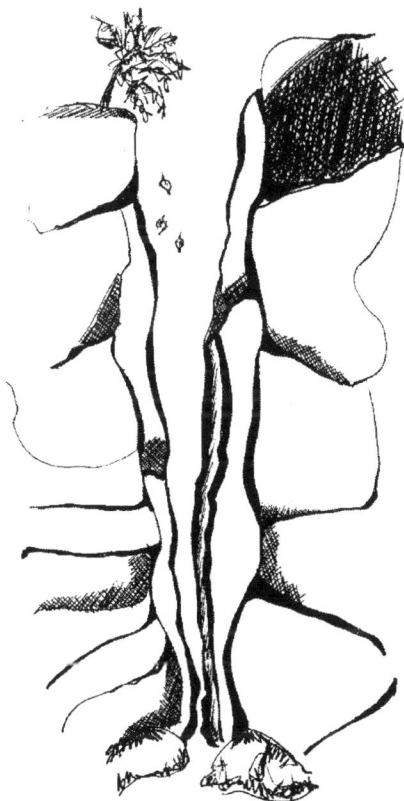

The Calling

The calling comes
> In the stillness of the night
> In the quiet moments of dawn when sun is
> rising
> In the recesses of the heart

The calling comes
> Unmistakable
> Certain
> Without words it dwells in the heart

The calling comes
> Heart's only response is spirit of willingness
> A soul surrendered
> A life placed on the altar

The calling comes
> Not bundled with worldly wealth
> But from a need to serve
> And a desire to fulfill Spirit's will

The call answered
> Go in response to Spirit
> Go and be blessed
> Go with Everlasting Arms sustaining

Victory

Victory do not elude me
Victory obtained through grit has temporal satisfaction
Victory that comes with roots reaching for water, is eternal

I stand at the crossroads
Shall I strive or shall I rest?
If I choose to strive – I will enter daily battle
Only to be hewn upon the dung hill of exhaustion

If I choose to rest while I walk
If I choose to rest as I labor
If I choose to rest as I serve
Then victory will come
Victory will rein and rain
Droplets refreshing and cool
Rain with joy
Rain peace upon the labor of hands given to Spirit's will
Victory granted for moments spent in rest
Victory known in heart and soul

Stained Glass Theology

Light streaming awakens soul
    Filtered by stained glass
    Prism's migration
    Colors mingle
    Vibrant blend
    Light diffused

Message streaming in colorful splendor
Awakened by the call to go
    Feed my lambs
    Clothe the naked
    Love the disenfranchised
Focus shifts
Incantations cease
Faith takes unsteady steps
A life lived to give

Emotions remain
Like ebb and flow of ocean's tide
Emotions grip the heart

Faith requires trust
Faith courts beliefs
Faith is substance without texture

Questions bubble to the surface
Live by emotions gripping heart?
Live by faith gripping soul?
Two separate spheres
Like oil and water
Cannot be fused

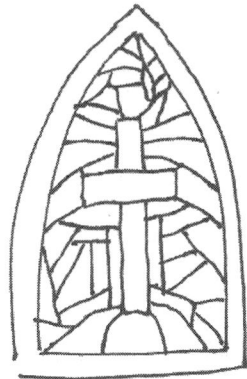

Cannot become one
Emotion calls us to experience life
Like a prairie landscape shifting with the seasons
Emotions come with eternal shifts
Like tall grass flowing with the rhythm of ocean waves under
summer sun
Autumn arrives, the grass withers to be claimed by earth's
rich soil
Snow blankets earth going into hibernation
Spring time stirs us from sleep
Emotions, the eternal circle twisting in our hearts

Faith stands in contrast
A call to action
To receive the love of God
Pour it out
      On others
      With others
      To others
Faith – invisible to the eye
Faith – seen through giving
Faith – pouring out what is given to us in love

Stained glass theology
Moved to give without encumbrance on the soul?
Moved to action without knowing outcome?
Do we respond to emotion's tug?
Do we respond to the mingle of faith and works?

The question remains in the cathedral of our stained glass
theology

I Come

Heart aflame – I come
Heart discouraged – I come
Heartbroken – I come
Whatever my state
I come
> To the foot of the cross
> To the mercy seat
> To sit under your wings

Protected
Shielded
Cradled

I come to receive
> Rivers of living water
> Bread of life
> Fruits of the spirit

I leave to
> Serve
> Comfort
> Heal
> Give
> See the face of God in others

But alas, I leave to love because I have been loved

Loss

Loss comes
Stealing away relationships
Leaving us isolated
    Alone in the wilderness of sadness and loss
Our hearts grieve
Our eyes – moist with tears of aloneness
Our minds ask, "Why?"
We move
    Robotically through murky waters
A cloud covers us
We seek relief, but none comes
So we move forward
Longing for restoration
But the chain of loss attached to the ball of regret slows
    down our journey
Shall we stop?
    To weep?
    To be swept away with regrets?
    To whine?
To stop is to welcome death into our hearts
To travel on an ill-defined road is to embrace hope and faith
The cross road of decision
Which way shall be chosen?

Brokenness

Angry waves batter soul
Frothy waves beat on breast
Waves in never ending flow
Claiming existence's being
High tide sweeps mind and heart into exhaustion's state

Lying on the shore
Face down in sand
Low tide ebbs
A sigh of relief breathing into grains of sand
No longer claimed by wave's angry grip

But I lie still
Battered from pounding waves
Stillness creeps in on cat's paws
Night approaches
Full moon rises above horizon

Moon, round and firm
Moon casting shadows of remorse
Shadows clinging to silent grains of sand
Sand echoes no reply
Soul is torn

Anguished soul cries out: "Deliver me."
Moon beckons
"Arise. Walk in the sands of time
Your relief comes at dawn
When the Son is revealed."

Section III:

Reflections on the Journey

Fishing

In night's darkness
When light is shaded
When silence covers the earth
I venture forth
Trolling my boat
Drop the net
Bring it up
     Nothing
     Empty
     Not one fish to behold

Drop the net
Bring it up
     Again
     And again
     And again
Nothing
Empty net
Not one fish
Much effort, but no fish
No sustenance
No food
Empty

Then He comes
Calling from the shore
"Drop the net" He calls out
So close to shore
Too close to shore
Surely no fish here
Hesitation means no victory

What is there to lose?
Drop the net
Pull it up
It is heavy beyond bearing
I cannot pull it up
Heavy with fish
Will the net hold?
I ask for help
Hands show up
Pull! Pull! Pull!
Fish beyond number

Wade to shore
He is there
Fish and bread prepared
And once again He feeds from the bounty

He asks, "Will you follow?"
"Yes"
He asks again, "Will you follow?"
"Of course, yes"
"Will you follow where I lead?"
"Yes! Yes! What more beyond Yes?"

It is complete
It shall be
United in will

An Inheritance

Inheritance received
Cannot be measured
Riches beyond gold's finest
We take hold of it
We possess it; we do not let go

Shall we build with it?
Should we bury it for safe keeping?
Will we squander it?

We hold tight to inheritance
To find emptiness in possession
Holding on only leaves emptiness

Richness can be found in inheritance
    Leave it behind for those who follow
    We leave for them what we have become
    Our true inheritance left to others
        is the gift of our victories won

Leaving inheritance to others
>   Not left to be measured and weighed
>   Not left to be spent
>   Not left to be possessed

The inheritance we leave
Comes from lessons learned
>   Painful roads traveled
>   Relationships rendered destroyed
>   Loss of the anticipated

Show our children how to live with inheritance
They will know how to face
>   Challenges
>   Blocked roads
>   Loss
>   Grief
>   Sorrow

Aloneness

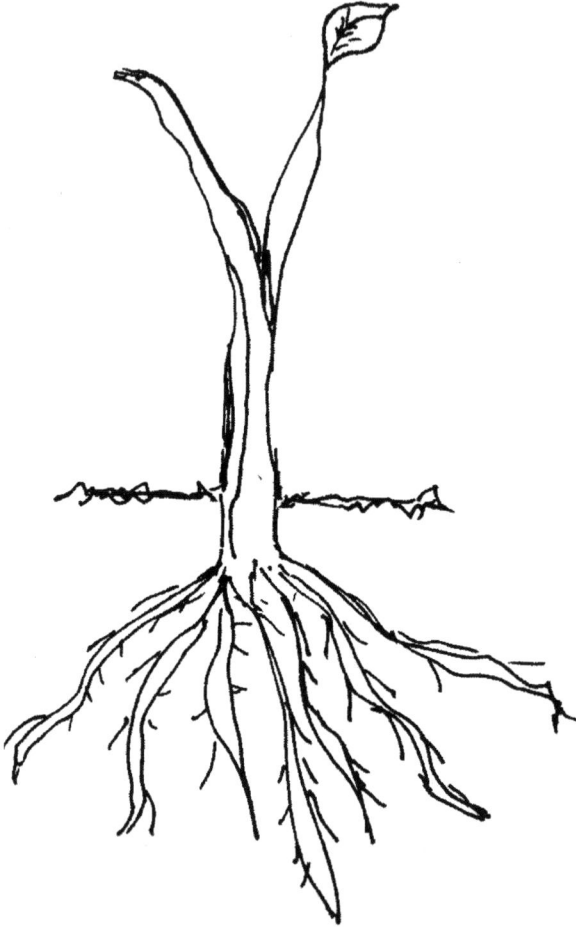

Loneliness touches not
Loneliness is temporary
Vanishing into space when void is filled with presence

But aloneness comes under the cover of darkness
Aloneness creeps into the bones

Aloneness seeps into the marrow of the soul
    Isolated
    Abandoned
    Betrayed

I cry out
Do you know broken hearted pain?
How much aloneness shall be borne?
It is not for the lack of friends
It is rooted in lack of
    Connection
    Empathy
    Love gone astray

My heart cries out another's presence
A presence not to fill the aloneness
But a presence
    To love
    To respect
    To honor
In search of connection
To give and receive unconditionally
    Friendship
    Creating oneness
    Producing solidarity

In friendship aloneness can rest
In our oneness aloneness melts
In solidarity aloneness finds remedy
Our hearts unite – for we are now one
Aloneness dissolves in the arms of true connectedness

We are Community

We are community
In breaking bread – your body broken
In drinking wine – your blood shed

Community extended
We recite creed
Say in unison, "Lord, hear our prayer"
Sing the mystery of our faith

Community becomes reality
Reality is community
When we see your presence
    In the friendless neighbor
    Beside the sick
    Assisting the poor
    Visiting the imprisoned
    Loving the disenfranchised

Community encompasses our being
    When love flows out
    Love flows in
    Then we are one

God in the Ordinary

God in the ordinary
    Washing dishes
    Cutting grass
    Comforting a child
    Laughing with a friend
    Earning our bread
God in the ordinary
    As bird takes flight
    When kitten purrs
    Eggs hatching
    Horses grazing
    Sunrise, sunset
God meets us in the ordinary
    Do we hear Him?
    Are we aware of His silent presence?
    Do we see His guiding hand?
    Are we secure in His loving embrace?
    Do we believe He sets the table before us?
God meets us in the ordinary
This is the opportunity to respond to His love
Then He anoints us with the extraordinary oil of joy, peace,
and gladness

Grace and Mercy

Grace and mercy, undivided duo
      Shedding light
      Bequeathing favor
      Giving blessing
      Bringing comfort
      Bestowing forgiveness

Rejoice in dual presence
Assured by undivided duo
Living in state of grace and mercy

The Journey and the Fog

The journey continues
A path lies before me unrevealed
Step by step
Fog: dense, damp and deep
Fog: Encircles, clouding vision
With each step a question haunts the soul
Will the next step be a misstep?
A misstep off a precipice
Into a void
A void with no hope for survival?
If I stop – no progress is made
If I stop – no lessons are learned
If I stop – faith eludes my soul

Hesitating
I take another step
It lands on rock ground
The voice comes
"I send my angels lest you dash your foot upon the rock."
"BUT!" I cry out
The voice encourages, "Take another step."
I hesitate – my mind whirls
This is insanity at its height

Then the angel engulfs with her wings
Another step
More rocks
My foot has not dashed against the rock's hardness
The fog has not lifted
But I see with new eyes
Can resurrection come without being encased in a rock
fortified tomb?

God in Everything

God in everything
Everything in God
God in the daily walk
God giving daily provisions
God always present

God in love
     with us
     for us
     in us

We are His beloved
We are the apple of His eye
We bask in His presence

God incarnate
     Speaking wisdom in parable
     Healing the lame
     Opening the eyes of the blind
     Resonating sound to the deaf
     Ultimate giving of body and blood

A holy residence He takes up
      Loving us
      Encompassing us
      Indwelling within
      Bringing comfort
      Giving sustenance

God in everything
      In every place
      In every circumstance
      In every person we meet

Surrender

Surrender to love
Love that poured out life
Love that sacrificed body and blood

The Hound of Heaven pursues
Walk. Jog. Run.
Pursuit intensifies
There is no escape
Except through surrender

Kick. Squeal. Struggle.
Exhausted
Surrender is the sole path
Enveloped in love
Surrender is sweet
Surrender is joy
Surrender means trust

"Your will be done"
"Your path is the way"
The only way
Surrender to love
Eat the bread of healing
Drink the sweet wine of acceptance
Only to surrender to love again
Afresh each day
To experience the joy anew with each sunrise

Flowers at the Altar

Ordinary time
Altar draped in green
Flowers brought as gift
Colorful radiant flowers
Green leaves matching green altar cloth

The altar
Symbol of sacrifice
Flowers left as gift

Host displayed
Ultimate sacrifice of
      Body
      Blood
      Life

Flowers and host blend
The sacrificed one accepts the flower gift
The sacrificed one gently holds gift and giver

      United
      Great mystery
      Gift and sacrifice are one

Year by Year

Year by year
Another ring
Years of drought
Years of rain's abundance
Time passes
Dormant in winter's rest
Giving chance for new ring to form

Just like tree
Reaching for sky
Our souls marked with rings
Times of drought
Times filled with abundance
Our core reflecting Spirit's rain

Eye Cannot Say

We gather together
Bringing talents
Arriving with personality
Formed by life's voyage across ocean's open waters
Each soul uniquely formed

Seeing
Hearing
Feeling
Knowing
Sensing

But eye cannot say, "All that is needed is sight."
Ear cannot say, "I hear; therefore, I know all."
Heart cannot say, "Because I feel I have no need for
    knowing."
Mind cannot say, "Knowledge conquers all."

Soul speaks out, "Understanding awakens compassion
        for our human bond"

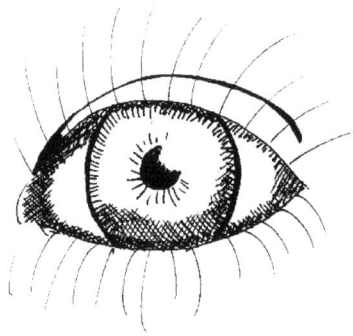

For when we mingle
Each brings
>Faith
>Race
>Heritage
>Culture
>Language

We are one
Created to be united
>To see the divine in others
>To hear voice of Spirit
>To feel another's joy and sorrow
>To know life's challenges and rewards
>To understand we are one

We are Gift

We are gift
Wrapped in life's journey

Two souls open
    Raw
    Wounded
    Betrayed
    Broken
    Bleeding
Two souls touch
    Holding the other's wounds
    Listening with heart
    Seeing with compassion

Together we sip wine pressed from the grapes of life
Bonds are forged
Bonds woven by giving and receiving
    Bonds stronger than steel
    Yet more gentle than a baby's embrace

Acceptance, tenderness, and love
    Intertwined
    Mingled with silent tears
    Pain held in sacred trust
The gift exchange begins

In giving – we receive
In receiving – we give
Unconditional love

No down payment required
No tally sheet kept
No action adjudicated

The love each desires is found in loving the other
A new journey begins
On a road without map

We are gift

About the Author

Juliana Peter is new to the writing and the publishing world. Her professional career has spanned five decades as an educator, corporate trainer, instructional designer, consultant and career coach. Always ready for something new as well as challenging, she is now launching into the world of creative writing.

She lives in Colorado with her husband and two mischievous (aren't they all mischievous?) cats. She enjoys cooking, curling up with a good book or working on a needlepoint project. When not engaged in an indoor activity, Juliana is out exploring the great outdoors; she is hiking, skiing, snow shoeing, cycling and occasionally accompanying her husband with a fly-fishing rod in hand.

Take a moment to like her on Facebook: @eagleswingsbooks.

She can be contacted for poetry readings at eagleswings@mail.com

About the Illustrator

Jill Benson Flanagan began drawing at a very young age. Her first drawings were on the walls in her house, much to the consternation of her mother. Her passion for painting emerged as an undergraduate student at Colorado State University (CSU). Today the subjects of her paintings include animals, architecture, landscapes, ocean views and still life. She holds a BFA from CSU.

Jill lives in Edwards, Colorado with her husband who encourages her to pursue her passion. On mountain trails, she is often accompanied by her bundle of furry love, an adorable Malamute.

For more information and to see Jill's paintings, her work can be viewed at www.jillbenson.com .

About the Cover's Photographer

John Dakin brings close to 40 years of career media operations experience to his role as Vice President of Communications for the Colorado Snowsports Museum in Vail, Colorado including work with the U.S. Ski Team, 1996 Olympic Summer Games and the 2002 and 2010 Olympic Winter Games. A native of Grand Junction, Colorado, John served as Vice President of Communications for the nonprofit Vail Valley Foundation from 1987 to 2015 helping to create, organize and produce the Foundation's annual athletic, cultural and educational events and programs, along with major international events, including the 1989, 1999 and 2015 FIS Alpine World Ski Championships and the 1994 and 2001 UCI World Mountain Bike Championships.

John spends his free time photographing wild life and birds in the Vail Valley in Colorado.

Made in the USA
San Bernardino, CA
17 September 2018